MW00959109

STEVEN DANIEL

RUNNING AT 60 AND OVER

5 keys to start and continue running after 60

Copyright © 2023 by Steven Daniel

All rights reserved. No part of this publication may be reproduced, stored or transmitted in any form or by any means, electronic, mechanical, photocopying, recording, scanning, or otherwise without written permission from the publisher. It is illegal to copy this book, post it to a website, or distribute it by any other means without permission.

Steven Daniel asserts the moral right to be identified as the author of this work.

Steven Daniel has no responsibility for the persistence or accuracy of URLs for external or third-party Internet Websites referred to in this publication and does not guarantee that any content on such Websites is, or will remain, accurate or appropriate.

Designations used by companies to distinguish their products are often claimed as trademarks. All brand names and product names used in this book and on its cover are trade names, service marks, trademarks and registered trademarks of their respective owners. The publishers and the book are not associated with any product or vendor mentioned in this book. None of the companies referenced within the book have endorsed the book.

First edition

This book was professionally typeset on Reedsy.
Find out more at reedsy.com

Contents

1

Introduction

Welcome to Running at 60 and After. My name is Steven Daniel and I am very excited to share the joys of running with you. I am a "regular runner", who enjoys the healthy lifestyle and benefits of running as my primary health and fitness routine. While I do not know how many years God has planned for me on this earth, I do believe running on a regular basis will enhance the years to come. I currently have a beautiful family that includes three grandsons. I believe running provides me with the health and energy I desire to get the most out of life driven by faith, family, fitness, focus, and fun.

During a conversation with colleagues, I was asked if I had big plans for the weekend. My reply was "Yes. Start my training schedule for a half marathon." First reply, "The only time you'll see me running is because someone is chasing me. Doesn't sound like fun to me." Second reply. "That's cool, but I can't even imagine myself running at this stage of life." Now, I am very confident that I was the only 60+ person in the conversation, but I proceeded to tell why I enjoy running. Especially, when I'm **not** being chased!!

That conversation, and many more like it in recent years, inspired me to write a simple, pragmatic book to encourage folks 60+ to consider running. I am 65 and love to run. I am not a professional or accomplished runner. Just a guy who loves the experience of a run. There is something about it that provides me with extraordinary energy and a sense of accomplishment every time I run. Whether I run two miles or ten miles, does not matter. It is more like going on an adventure than getting in a workout. Though I typically run similar routes, I see new things, new faces, and enjoy different points of reflection on almost every run. I have a playlist with some of my favorite tunes that enhance the experience. I do not use music to set the pace for my run, or inspire me to run. I just listen to the words and tunes of the songs and try to sing along, while focusing on my form. In fact, singing with the songs actually helps me be mindful of my breathing, which helps me manage my form. More on form later.

If you have never run before, or it has been many years since you last ran, you will likely raise a few eyebrows among family and friends. I have been running for several years, with some of those years more committed and productive and some not so committed. In the committed and productive years, I take a few jabs from family and friends. "Run, Forest Run"1, "Let's go Flash", etc. As with anything in life, when we take up new things, even those closest to us may not understand, or be supportive. While my family and friends may think I am crazy for running at my age, they all appreciate the fact that I do not look and act sixty-five. Whether or not I look sixty-five, I feel very much like I did a decade ago. Maybe a few minor aches and pains, but I am healthy, energetic, and able to enjoy life and I attribute it to a few things. Faith, family, fitness, focus, and fun. Running checks three of the boxes for me, and allows me to maintain commits to both faith and family. Bottom-line for me, running is fun and enjoyable.

Running must be fun for other 60 and over Americans, because it continues to grow in popularity among seniors. Over the last 25 Years, the New York City Marathon has seen a 4000% increase in runners over the age of 65. The intent of this book is **not** to train 60 and over marathoners. The basic intention is to raise awareness of the benefits of a healthy lifestyle and provide a simple way to incorporate the pleasures of running. The less basic intention is the hope that I may encourage at least one person to take up running and enjoy a similar experience as mine.

Throughout the book, I will reference websites, apps, and products I found over the years that help me enjoy my passion for running. They are not included for promotion, but examples of things I use that allow me to stay committed to running in hopes I can someday write a sequel, 'Running at 90 and Over'. If you are new to running, I am certain you will explore and find those things that work well for you. If you are currently a runner, you may already have some favorites. Thanks to technology, the websites, apps, and products available to enhance your running experience are countless. Being a creature of habit, my family calls my 'system', those I reference have been part of my 'system' for several years. Odds are, I will not likely explore others unless My 'system' things are no longer available.

Since I have not been very successful in influencing family and friends to become regular runners, let's get going and see if I can influence **YOU** to take up the activity and become a regular runner!

2

Can I Run?

Yes, maybe, or no. The three options. *Yes I can* run means you have the desire and are willing to put forth the effort. For you, I hope this book will serve as a simple guide for encouragement and direction.

Maybe I can run means you have the ability, just not certain if you have the desire and willingness to take the plunge. For you, I hope this book will inspire you to give running a shot.

No I cannot run means you are not able to run, due to a physical or medical reason. If you are physically or medically unable to run, there are still options for you to enjoy and I will provide a real-life example and some suggestions on how running can be part of your life.

According to a report by the **Sports & Fitness Industry Association**, there are more than **47 million** runners and joggers in the United States, more than half of whom run at least once per week. Personally, I do not distinguish between running and jogging. I have been told a runner's pace is under 10 minutes per mile, while a jogger's pace is greater than 10 minutes per mile. Let me say that a 10 mile run at 10:01 per mile is a run for me. When I first started running regularly, a 1.5 mile run at 12 minutes per mile was a run, not a jog! At 65, any run for me over 5 miles is a run, regardless of the pace. Now I am competitive and I do like to run at a 'runner's' pace. My aim is to not lay that burden on you, as we go forward, but help you get started on your running journey and provide some tips that will help you enjoy the experience.

So, who is running? 55.9 million people participated in a running-based activity in the U.S. Again, 'Over the last 25 years, the New York City Marathon has seen a 4000% increase runners over the age of 65. There are a lot of people running and the 65+ group numbers are increasing at one of the world's most famous running events. It seems that many people are running and the number of 65+ competitive runners is a growing population. I previously stated the intent of this book is **not** to train 60 and over marathoners. However, this is such a remarkable statistic, I felt compelled to include it one more time. Preparing for a marathon is a feat. Less than 1% of the population in the U.S. has completed a Marathon, according to RunRepeat. Basically, less than 3.3 million of the 55.9 million U.S. runners completed a marathon leaving the remainder as participants in other run-based activities. Without getting into the weeds with data, let's agree there are millions of runners who are regular runners and about 3% of those are senior runners. I would estimate the number to be approximately 1.5 million. That is a lot of runners my age and older!

A lot of senior runners, logging a lot of miles. Basically, the *yes I can run* group should get after it. The *maybe I can run* group should give it a go, and the *no I cannot run* group should consider the following if they are interested but not able. Chair exercises, adaptive running, walking, or swimming are a few low-to-no impact exercises to consider. One could also attend running events as a spectator or volunteer to experience the fun and fellowship of racing.

There is a father-son duo who took participation to a different level. Dick Hoyt and his son Rick Hoyt are a famous father-son duo who have participated in numerous marathons and triathlons together. Rick was born with cerebral palsy and is quadriplegic, but that did not stop him from participating in these events. Dick pushed Rick in a specialized wheelchair during the races. The duo completed 32 Boston Marathons together, until Dick retired in 2014 citing health reasons. Dick died in 2021, but you can see the joy Rick had when racing with his dad through the link in the resources.

This is an extraordinary story of the love between father and son and the love of running. It is a bond between two people that love running with very different capabilities and an inspiration to me to enjoy the gift of ability as long as I am able.

With the desire to participate, running is not cost-prohibitive either. Compared to other fitness activities, running possibly has the most affordable entry level cost. Of course, the cost could vary based on your location and climate, due to clothing requirements in colder climates. At its very basic level of entry, in temperate climates, a good pair of shoes, shirt, and shorts can get you started. As with any fitness activity, one can spend as much money as they want. For a beginning runner, I recommend a t-shirt, sport shorts, and a comfortable pair of shoes. If you find running to be your thing, you can up the ante. Until then, throw on a t-shirt, a pair of shorts, and shoes and get out there and run!!

3

Is running good for me?

R unning has many health benefits. According to WebMD, running can help improve heart health. Lower the risk of cardiovascular disease, improve sleep quality, improve knee and back health, improve memory, trigger your immune system, and boost your mood and energy. For me, running is the most effective way to maintain my metabolism, weight, and body mass index (BMI). Running also, when done well and with proper shock absorption, can be an excellent method for bone building.

Running has many emotional benefits. According to a report by John Hopkins Medicine, running can help reduce anxiety, depression, and stress. Running can also improve mood and self-confidence, and promote feelings of relaxation and well-being. Research shows that running can lead to the release of endocannabinoids, which are mood-improving neuromodulators that promote short-term psychoactive effects such as reduced anxiety and feelings of calm. Running can also help improve cognitive function, including memory and focus.

In addition to the short-term benefits, regular cardiovascular exercise such as running can spark growth of new blood vessels to nourish the brain. Exercise may also produce new brain cells through a process called neurogenesis, which may lead to an overall improvement in brain performance and prevent cognitive decline.

While I prefer to run alone, because it is fun for me and is often a time for self-reflection. Sort of a non-quiet time quiet-time. Also, I have never found a runner with the same pace, stride, and rhythm. Could be that I have no rhythm!! Truthfully, on runs greater than 5 miles, I regularly alter my stride and pace. There are a variety of reasons for doing this, but it is really just part of my 'system'. So, it is just easier and more enjoyable to run on my own.

For many runners, there are a number of social benefits to running. Running with a partner or group can provide motivation and account-ability to stick to a routine. Running groups and clubs can provide opportunities to meet new people and make friends. Others can provide emotional support and encouragement, especially on challenging runs or races. Running with others can make running more enjoyable and fun, or provide opportunities for friendly competition and help improve performance. The *maybe I can run* group might gain the most from running with others and the social benefits of doing so. Motivation, support, and encouragement may be the missing ingredient to get you started and keep you in the game.

4

5 keys to start and continue running after 60

While the book is focused on starting and continuing to run after 60, these keys have kept me in the game and relatively injury-free for over three decades. They have been the keys to getting me back into this thing I truly enjoy, when I put it on the back burner. Unlike other exercise activities, running is a full-body workout. Lungs, heart, upper body, abs, legs, and brain are all important to an enjoyable running experience. The following are what I consider to be essential to a life with running as a fitness staple.

Talk to your doctor!

a clean bill of health

Running is a whole body workout. Therefore, it is important, if not critical, that every runner discuss their plans with their primary care provider. Whether you are considering running for the first time, increasing from occasional running to regular running, or preparing for a race, have the conversation with a medical provider. Like many who will read this book, I would be considered a consumer of healthcare. I work in the healthcare industry, but I am not a clinician. However, I am close enough to the clinical side of healthcare that I probably consume less because I know just enough to be dangerous. (Not to others, but to myself!) I have a tendency to self-diagnose and, because I am in fairly good shape, tend not to ask a lot of questions or offer information that 'feels' a bit trivial.

Because of these tendencies, a visit to my primary care provider is the first and most important key to start and continue running after 60.

For that matter, any age. The human body is amazingly designed. So many parts, systems, and functions working in sync to enable us to do so many things. Breathe, eat, drink, sleep, think, see, walk, talk, hear, etc. So many more design details enable us to live our lives. If one or more are not working properly, even the most basic activities can be challenging, or impossible. I believe running challenges the majority of the parts and functions of the human body and requires, at the very least, a professional to review them prior to and in support of our running experience. Please understand, I personally have to force myself to embrace the concept of including regular check-ups in my plans for running. I more often lean to the philosophy of 'If it's not broken, don't fix it!'

Because of the complexity of the human body, we may not know when some part, system, or function is not working properly. As stated previously, running stresses the whole body and finding out on a run that something is not working or is fragile is not the right time or place. There are no money back guarantees the most advanced healthcare and science can identify and prevent failure during a run. However, the odds of finding out during a run are much less likely if you involve your healthcare provider in your running experience plans. Because of my work in the healthcare industry I know this, and sometimes see the devastating results of folks not including regular check-ups in their life's plans. Consider the following analogy.

While serving in the United States Navy (many years ago), I had the pleasure of flying on the P-3 Orion platform. Hunted and tracked submarines for a living. Best job ever!! And, probably a story, or stories for another time and another book.

11

While I was not a pilot, my primary job duties were in the aircraft while flying. I loved to fly and loved to hunt and track submarines. Every successful mission was dependent on a fully functional, safe aircraft. On the ground before and after every flight, there were a multitude of tests and checklists performed to assess the flight-worthiness of the aircraft. Once the aircraft was deemed ready for flight, the plane was available for us to fly. Before, during, and after every mission, the flight crew recorded and reported any unusual events related to the aircraft. If there were none, the aircraft was handed over to the maintenance team for regular checks and maintenance. If there were any unusual events. The aircraft was grounded, and not allowed to be used for a flight until the issue was resolved, or damage repaired.

Regular checks, maintenance, and repairs were not the responsibility of the flight crew. While we had some knowledge of the aircraft as a whole, we relied upon the expertise of highly trained experts to assess, diagnose, and repair the aircraft for flight readiness. While it was a pain in the backside to have a mission delayed, canceled, or aircraft change, we respected and appreciated their expertise and work that allowed me and my fellow air crewmen to complete our mission and return home safely.

Because I am not a clinician, I often relate my body to an aircraft. A highly sophisticated vessel designed to do extraordinary things. As with the P-3 Orion, I know what my body was designed to do and have little better than general knowledge of how it works. I also know what I do not know. I do not know what goes on inside and out of my body that could or could not cause failure. Like the team I flew with in the Navy, who just wanted to fly, I just want to take off running and do what I love to do. However, as much as it feels like a bother, I know I must rely upon the expertise of a highly trained professional to give clearance to allow me to enjoy the experience of running and to do it for the long haul.

The key is to get a regular check-up before you start and as you continue to run. Report and discuss any health and physical issues or concerns you have to your medical provider. Then, you are ready to plan your running journey!!

Have a plan

Now that you have cleared your body to get started, let's get to planning. Planning any workout is vital to successful outcomes. While running might seem to be an easier exercise activity to start than most, many runners experience injuries every year. While the vast majority of these injuries are minor and do not prevent participants from continuing their journey, most are avoidable with the discipline of planning and executing the plan.

Including 1-3 days of cross-training is advisable. At a minimum, I recommend core exercises, and upper body strengthening. Both are essential to endurance and running form, which will be discussed later in this chapter. Many runners incorporate leg exercises and most coaches recommend it. For me, I focus exclusively on the upper body and core. There are many websites and other materials for reference on the pros and cons for supporting your running plan, and most come with recommendations. For the beginner, I believe it is more important to have a plan to get you started running. As your activity increases, you further develop a plan that suits your needs and goals.

Let's plan our running journey. A simple approach to planning should include a long-term goal, key milestones, measurements of success, realistic targets, stretch milestones, and timelines for each milestone. My current plan is to run a half-marathon. It is a twelve week plan and the long-term goal is to complete it with an average pace of under 10 minutes. For some this may seem like a lofty goal, while to others it might seem a bit underwhelming.

For me, I have not run a half-marathon since 2015. While I am a regular runner, 13.1 miles is a long run and I was eight years younger when I last ran the distance. The long-term goal is to complete the race. The plan is detailed to include weekly milestones with distance and speed targets. For me, distance is more important than pace, so I work to complete the planned distance for each week. The distance is realistic and the pace is a bit of a stretch. The timeline is specific. The race date is set and I am registered. Have a plan and work on it daily. When the race is finished, I will set a plan for my regular running schedule. It will include some new routes, different distances, and possibly a few 5K fun runs for the social benefits of running.

As stated in the introduction, I will reference some websites, apps, and products I use to enhance my running experience. For races and my regular running plans, I use the app Run with Hal.10 I use the Run with Hal+ version, because the plan is modified each week based on the previous week's performance and can be adjusted if my schedule changes. The plus version has a modest fee, but the basic app is free. If you do want to use the app, his website Hal Higdon - Time-Tested Training Programs for Marathons & More provides a great deal of information and resources. There are many other options for training and planning available, but I am a creature of habit and have been using Hal's website and app for several years. The most important point is to develop a plan!

If you are a beginner, your plan may be to get started. You may not have any idea what the long-term looks like, but know you want to start running. So you long-term plan may be as follows:

Goal
　　Run 3 days per week for 2 months

Milestones (you may alternate running and walking each of the 3 days)
　　Week 1 - Run/walk .25 miles
　　Week 2 - Run .25 miles
　　Week 3 - Run .25 miles, walk .25 miles
　　Week 4 - Run .5 miles[insert running photo]
　　Week 5 - Run .5 miles, walk .25 miles
　　Week 6 - Run .75 miles
　　Week 7 - Run .75 miles, walk .25 miles

Week 8 - Run 1 mile

<u>Realistic</u>
Run at least .5 miles, run/walk 1 mile

<u>Stretch</u>
Run 1 mile

<u>Timeline</u>
2 months

For a beginner, this plan may be too aggressive. For a very active person, it may not be a stretch, or even challenging. For all, it is not the content of the plan that is important. Having a plan is most important. You will have to determine the plan that is best for you at your current level of health and fitness. Heck, you may only be able to walk a quarter of a mile and running 50 feet might be your 2 month goal. If accountability is an issue, invite a friend or family member to be your accountability partner. Whether they join you or not, they can serve as a source of encouragement, inspiration, and support. **The key is to develop a plan and start executing.** Now you have a plan and are ready to fuel the plan?

Fuel your run

Running consumes a lot of energy. It works out every part of your body. Most regular runners are typically thinner than others whose fitness routines are of a higher priority. It does not mean that you will be 'skinny' if you run. For me, I am not certain I would enjoy running if the aim was weight control. I would likely lose interest, as many do with dieting and other weight-loss strategies. For what it is worth, I believe the primary purpose for running is the experience. Because running consumes a lot of energy, it requires fuel.

Food and water are essential fuels for runners. This may seem like a no-brainer, but I am often amazed how many times I have not been up for a run because I do not have enough fuel in the tank. For me, planning my meals and liquid intake is more important than planning my run. While serving in the Navy, fitness became a passion of mine. To fuel the passion, I found that not letting myself get hungry was an essential part of my fitness plan. This is one of those 'systems' my family often 'lovingly' refer to. I normally eat six times per day, 3 meals and 3 snacks, and try to drink at least 64 ounces of water. If I run in the morning, breakfast and mid-morning snacks are essential. If I do add fuel to an empty tank, I will not be able to recover properly from the run, and will not have the energy I need to enjoy my day. If I run in the late-afternoon, early evening, the mid-afternoon snack is key. Fuel helps me focus and supports my endurance. Regardless of what time of day I run, water is critical. Because I live on the Gulf Coast, I often supplement my hydration with an electrolyte replacement. My preferred drinks are powdered, pre-measured serving packets, lower in sodium, and without caffeine and sugar. Most importantly, the body can endure a bit of hunger, but insufficient water intake can be dangerous.

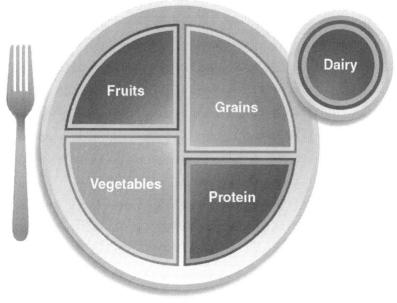

Choose**MyPlate**.gov

Meal and liquid planning **should** be part of your running plan. Take the time to plan food and hydration for all running activities. I recommend writing the plan and planning shopping to support the plan, until your diet and consumption become habits. Over time, the fuel requirements to support your running plan(s) will become almost second nature. I encourage you to be creative with your meal plans, while focusing on the quality of the foods you choose to eat. I find that foods with less fat burn cleaner and provide better energy to support my running plan. Consuming higher levels of plants and complex carbs better support my running, and moderate protein intake works best for me. I try to stay at a consistent weight, with a range of +- 5 pounds to get the most out of my running plan. This is not a dieting plan, but a meal planning approach to provide the right fuel for your plan. There are many resources available to provide you with more in depth knowledge to build your plan. **The key is to plan your meals and hydration to support your running plan and execution.** You are cleared to run, you have a running plan, and you have a plan to fuel your run. Ready to execute?

Focus on form versus distance and speed

For my current half-marathon plan, distance is more important than speed. When I get the distance down, I will work on the speed. However, to avoid injury and delays to my training, it is most important for me to focus on form. I am a heavy runner and distance running does not come naturally. Over the years, I have tried just about every technique and form to transform my running style, so that I can glide through a run or race like the professional runners. Not going to happen! What I have been able to do is find a 'system' that works well for me.

Several years ago, a physician friend and triathlete, observed me running. Our training schedules caused us to cross paths every Saturday morning. Over lunch one afternoon, he asked if I was having pain and/or struggles during my runs. I told him yes and felt like the half-marathon I was training for would likely be my last and I wasn't sure I would be able to continue my goal of being a lifetime runner. He explained that it appeared as though I were running with my body straight up and down, appearing to almost be leaning back. I was and it was intentional. Because I had been battling shin splints, I had adjusted my form to generate a heel-toe strike as my feet met the ground. This was creating heavy pressure on my hips and lower back and a lot of post-run pain and discomfort. He offered some advice which, over 10 years later, I can say is the number one reason I am running today and enjoying the blessing of being able to do so.

Chi Running, he explained, changed his knowledge and understanding of running. He adjusted his form and was running faster and freer than ever before. He suggested I read the book Chi Running, by Danny Dreyer. I did as he suggested and have been running regularly since reading the book. In fact, I have the Chi Running app and use it regularly to this day to remind me to focus on my form and pre-run warm-up and post-run routines. This is not a sponsored plug for Chi Running, but a thank you to Danny Dreyer, for introducing the knowledge to the world, and to my friend for introducing me to this run-saving philosophy and form. I encourage you, whether you are a beginner, or regular runner, to pay very close attention to your form. Form should take precedence over distance and speed. Over the long haul, you will only be able to increase distance and speed, if your body is properly absorbing the impact of running.

Injury-free running is determined by the form and efficiency of each of your running activities. When I feel discomfort, or unusually fatigued at any point during a run, I will slow down to a walking pace, make the mental adjustment to my form and start running again with great focus on maintaining form until I get back in rhythm. My aim is not to conquer each run, but to be able to enjoy a lifetime of running. **The key to executing your running plan and continuing running after 60 is to focus on form!** Cleared, planned, fueled, and managed form! Time to enjoy your run!!

Enjoy your run!

Enjoying your run! The absolute most important outcome of running. There are so many side benefits to running, but delight is the reason I continue to run. There are a few things that enhance my experience, but they are completely unnecessary to get the satisfaction I receive from running. Music is important, but it only enhances the experience. Some of my most efficient and best running activities have been on days, where I forgot my headphones, or they were not sufficiently charged. As previously mentioned, I listen to music for pleasure, not to aid in my cadence or provide encouragement. I simply love music and running and it is nice to enjoy them at the same time.

Advances in technology add a new dimension to my running experience. I am an Apple™ user and really enjoy the Apple Watch SE 2nd gen. With it, I can connect to my headset, listen to music, and track my progress on each run. It provides milestone updates for distance and pace and I do not have to have my phone with me. Really enhances the running experience. There are many technology options available for Apple and android users. I am certain you can find some that will enhance your experience.

Map out your route. Especially, if you are planning to run when it is dark, or low-light. I will typically take one of my rest days to walk a new route, or the portion of an extended route I have not yet run. It is very helpful to note road, trail, or sidewalk conditions prior to going out for a run. Nice to know if there are any places with standing water, or dogs that might change your race to a chase! Also, if you are running in the dark hours of the day, wear reflective materials or lighted vests or devices. Never assume drivers are expecting runners on their driving journey!

Dress for the temperature you expect when you finish the run versus the start of the run. Layers for colder weather, sun-protection for those sun-filled days. Especially for longer runs. If you feel it will help you relax and not worry about the heat, take some water or hydration supplement.

For runs less than eight miles, I drink prior to the run. Eight miles and over, I take fluids with me.

Warm-up and cool down!! I adhere to the Chi Running pre and post running event recommendations. Limbering movements before, with stretching and leg-drain after. This works very well for me, but I encourage you to explore and find what works best for you.

Smile!! Running should be comfortable and pleasing enough to bring a smile to your face! I can assure you I will not be smiling every time I run. However, I will do my absolute best to remind myself to smile.

Have fun! Fun is a mood for finding or making amusement. Get in the mood and find amusement in running!!

5

Let's get started!!

I highly recommend you create a checklist to use before every run, whether you are a beginner or experienced runner. Nothing is worse than forgetting something and figuring it out during your run. Hat, watch, phone, earphones, hydration, pre-run and/or post-run routine, etc.

Develop your plan. Write it down. Get a free template off a website. Use an app. Buy a book. Whatever works best for you, build your plan. There are many resources to help you plan your running activities and weekly routines. I found those that appealed directly to what I wanted to accomplish

Finally, execute your plan. If you struggle with consistency, find a family member or friend who can help. Just get started and tweak the plan as you go. I am thankful everyday that I am able to run and enjoy it. I hope the same for you. God willing, we will meet again in the sequel – Running at 90 and After!!

Thanks for choosing to read Running at 60 and After. I hope you enjoyed it and are inspired to become a regular runner. Please leave a review on Amazon. I would really like to know your thoughts and feedback. Have a wonderful run!!

6

Resources

Quote from the movie Forest Gump, 1994

How to Start (and Keep!) Running After Age 60 - Competitive Edge (compedgept.com. compedgept.com. Published July 7, 2021. Accessed October 29, 2023. https://compedgept.com/blog/running-after-sixty/

10+ Running Statistics You Need To Know In 2023 - 16best. 16best.net. Published March 14, 2023. Accessed October 29, 2023. https://www.16best.net/running-statistics-and-facts/

126 Running Statistics You Need to Know. livestrong.com. Published October 3, 2023. Accessed October 29, 2023. https://www.livestrong.com/article/13730338-running-statistics

Dick Hoyt, who pushed son in multiple Boston Marathons, dies. nbcnews.com. Published March 18, 2021. Accessed October 29, 2023. https://www.nbcnews.com/news/us-news/dick-hoyt-who-pushed-s

on-multiple-boston-marathons-dies-n1261397

Health Benefits of Running. webmd.com. Published July 18, 2023. Accessed October 29, 2023. https://www.webmd.com/fitness-exercise /health-benefits-running

The Truth Behind 'Runner's High' and Other Mental Benefits of Running. hopkinsmedicine.org. Accessed October 29, 2023. https://w ww.hopkinsmedicine.org/health/wellness-and-prevention/the-truth -behind-runners-high-and-other-mental-benefits-of-running

Mental Health Benefits of Jogging and Running. verywellfit.com. Published November 21, 2021. Accessed October 29, 2023. https://w ww.verywellfit.com/the-mental-benefits-of-jogging-2911666

Time-tested training from the renowned runner, author, and coach. halhigdon.com. Accessed October 29, 2023. https://www.halhigdon.c om/

CHI Running = Running never felt this good. chiliving.com. Published November 21, 2021. Accessed October 29, 2023. https://chiliving.com/ chirunning/

Made in the USA
Las Vegas, NV
28 December 2024

15519825R00017